FIRING GOD

FIRING GOD

Cheryl Abram

NON-DUALITY PRESS

NON-DUALITY PRESS | PO Box 2228 | Salisbury | SP2 2GZ
United Kingdom

ISBN: 978-1-908664-48-8

www.non-dualitypress.org

ACKNOWLEDGMENTS

All my love and gratitude go to:
My babies, Jared, Naomi, Paul and Daniel
for giving me motherhood and coloring my life
with tears, laughter and love

My siblings, Darlene, Gary, Marlene and Trisa
for being the most wonderful, thoughtful and
supportive siblings in all the universe

My mom Patricia for your courage, beauty
and divine presence

My friends and colleagues Julie Brill,
Cassie Brennand, Cindy Reynolds, Yadira Guerrero
and Jaye Murray for always being an amazing team,
politely laughing at my jokes, forgiving my
"twisted" since of humor, and tolerating
my chronic forgetfulness

CONTENTS

Part 1

FINDING MY WAY HOME

My life was falling apart in a thousand different ways and I could do nothing about it. Problems were around every corner, under every bush and behind every door and I was powerless against them.

I grew tired of reading inspiring books, uplifting books, encouraging books—books that, in the past, had given me hope. They were written by people who had experienced obstacles—disasters even—in their lives; they lived to tell the tale of how they overcame their difficulties and found fulfillment. I grew tired of waiting for that day when I would be telling my own story of triumph and happiness. I knew who I was, what my talents were, who I wanted to become and how I was supposed to reach my goals. I had an educational plan, a spiritual plan, a family plan, and many examples of successful black women who had what I wanted. So what was the problem? Why couldn't I achieve the happiness that I was working so hard for?

I grew up as a Christian (Southern Baptist) so I knew God's general plan for my life. As I understood it, I had to obtain salvation, suffer, sacrifice, die, and then go to heaven. There could be occasional happiness somewhere in that process, especially since I was a "believer", but it wasn't guaranteed. The only guarantee in this life was suffering but suffering was inevitable whether you were a Christian or not. No one escaped.

However, as a Christian, I was suffering for a good reason. I was suffering because I was special, set apart, divinely chosen and destined for heaven. At the age of twelve, when my suffering amounted to headaches, cramps and the occasional disagreement with my mom, being "special" was worth it. But by the time I was 35 I began to question whether being special was worth the suffering I had to endure. I began to wonder why life was so hard.

Why did living require so much effort? It really didn't make any sense. Even though I knew I was "supposed" to suffer or that "everybody has problems and it's the price you pay for living on this earth", I could no longer accept that. I didn't care that "Jesus suffered and he never sinned" or "sacrifice is required for eternal life". I didn't care about any of that and I began questioning whether it was really true— or not.

Either way, I wanted out of this prison of problems and this mental asylum of suffering. My solutions in the form of Christianity and my own ideas and choices were not working. I had to find my way out but I didn't know how.

When I began this journey, the goal was to be happy. I just wanted to be free of all, or most of, my problems. I wanted to wake up in the morning excited to see another day instead of dreading what that day would bring. I wanted to go through the day enjoying life instead of wondering how I was going to solve a current problem. I wanted to go to bed with a peaceful mind instead of being lulled to sleep by swirling thoughts of regret and worry.

Just one deep inhalation of peace would clear, or at least dilute the thick, choking fog of relationship problems, financial problems, emotional problems, psychological problems and physical problems. Then I would be able to tell *my* story about the way I'd improved and the things I'd gained that led to my peace and happiness.

I could be a role model for other individuals, especially African American women, who were going through the same kinds of hardships and were seeking to live a happier life. They would find courage and inspiration from my book; this book. It was a good plan; a proven plan. Now, as I write this, I know that I will never tell that story, I will never write that book. My plan to solve my problems never panned out.

The drive to overcome life's obstacles and be a role model for other women is no more. I never did improve myself and I failed to become a better person. I did not gain anything, but lost everything. I will never find the happiness I was looking for and I'm grateful for that every single day.

This book is written from where I am now; which is where I've always been. All my plans are still in place: I'm just no longer depending on those plans to make me happy or to save me. Nothing has really changed. If there is a difference then it's solely a difference in perspective. I was living my life as a character in a story rather than as the author. As the character I only knew and cared about my role and what I could get out of the story. As the author, I know all the characters and I know why they do the things they do. I know this because, as the author, I *am* all the characters. As the character, the problem was my inability to find a lasting solution. As the author, I see that the problem is not my inability to find a solution; the problem is my unquestioned belief in problems.

Chapter 1

The Beginning

As an adult I was hardly ever grateful. While gratefulness was a word thrown around in church and at home, I certainly didn't practice it very much; unless there was clearly something to give thanks for like more money, a new job, a better relationship, a new house or car, a new day, good health or some other very clear reason to be grateful. Gratitude for no apparent reason was simply ridiculous. Besides, I didn't have time for it—even when I should have been grateful. Life was all about solving problems and getting more. Problems were ever-present so getting more of anything (education, status, money, confidence) to help solve my problems was the fuel that propelled me through each day.

When it came to problem solving and getting more, church and God were the big players in my life. From a very young age, God was woven throughout every aspect of my existence, whether I wanted Him there or not.

I grew up in Bourg, Louisiana, on a plantation called Pecan Grove with my mom and her parents, Helen and Frederick. My grandfather, grandmother, aunts, uncles and cousins all lived on the plantation in various houses and trailers.

I had a wonderful childhood. My grandfather had a small farm with pigs, chickens and cows. He also had a huge garden with tomatoes, cucumbers, watermelons, corn and other vegetables. In addition to the garden plants we had a Japanese plum tree, a couple of fig trees, enormous pecan trees, blackberry bushes, mulberry trees and a myriad of other delicious things that grew in prickly bushes or fell from the trees. The plantation was next to a bayou, so fish, crab, shrimp and turtle were commonly on the dinner table.

My cousins and I would spend the day catching dragonflies (or mosquito hawks as we'd call them), running through the pasture, playing in the woods, and simply enjoying the hot and humid Louisiana days and nights. I had everything I needed. I had no problems.

In addition to the joy-filled playful times, I remember going to church. Church seemed to be a big deal because we went every Sunday. Going to church was not as fun as being with my cousins and playing outside in the rain. I didn't like to go. Church was boring and the benches were hard. I could understand going on holidays, but why did I have to go every Sunday and sometimes during the week?

It didn't seem as if *anyone* wanted to go to church. Whenever it was mentioned it was, "We *have* to go to church tomorrow". And when we didn't have to go, there was much cheering from the children and a tone of guilt, or something like it, in the voice of the adult explaining the reasons why he or she wasn't going either.

But those church reprieves were few and far between. Most Sundays I was there sitting on the rock-hard benches next to my mom, waiting for it to be over. On good days, I'd just fall asleep. When I was able to remain awake, I remember the songs, the long prayers and my uncle or another minister yelling really loudly from the pulpit.

Church wasn't all bad though. The one aspect of church I did like was the new church dress and shoes I would get for the holidays. On Christmas and Easter, church was not an obligation, it was something I anticipated. On those days I got to wear a beautiful new dress, white ruffled socks and patent leather shoes. With my freshly coiffed hair and a tiny handbag filled with tissue and candy, I would sit in church like a regular congregant and stay awake for most of the sermon. Other than that, if there weren't presents, candy or new clothes involved, church was a bust. On the obligatory church days I would wish I was at my other grandmother's house (my father's mother). She never went to church.

My other grandmother was Gladys but we called her "Gamula". We called her that because my oldest sister couldn't say "grandmother" when she was young, so as each of us came along, we all just called her Gamula. Gamula was my father's mother and I absolutely adored her. I loved all of my family but Gamula was special—and not just because she didn't make me go to church. I don't remember everything about her, like specific things she said, or the way her voice sounded, but I do remember feeling completely loved and protected when I was with her.

Gamula lived in Houma, a city a few miles away from Bourg. I loved going to Gamula's house. There was no bayou, pasture, farm animals or mulberry trees, but I did get to see my dad and my many friends in the neighborhood. Gamula kept all my toys in a box on her porch. As soon as I'd get to her house, I'd make a beeline for the box and begin rooting around for a new toy that I knew she or my dad had placed there. However, most days I'd abandon my toys on the porch, hop on my Big Wheel, and ride up and down the sidewalk from dawn till dusk. There was a lady on the corner who sold delicious sweet and salty snacks like pecan candy, brownies, chic-o-sticks, pickles, chips and frozen cups, so Gamula would always give me money to buy one or more treats.

I also remember someone coming every day to deliver hot food to Gamula. Every meal came with a delicious dessert that she would always share with me. I really knew my grandmother loved me because those desserts were surely created in heaven and only made for angels to consume. My theory was while it may have been created in a heavenly realm, the occasional crumb was permitted to fall to earth where it would take the form of chocolate cake, apple pie, blackberry dumplings and other sweet culinary delights. And who else but an angel disguised as a loving grandmother would have access to such a treasure and choose to share her special dessert with me?

I don't remember going to church at all when I was at Gamula's house, but that was fine by me. I felt more comfort, safety, awe and compassion when I was with Gamula than I'd ever felt in church. In fact, I'd never felt any of those things in church. Leaving Gamula's house was always a sad occasion.

Her death was even sadder. Gamula was my church—a church with a warm lap, soft, weathered brown skin, white hair and smiling eyes. Church was not a distant building with a humongous statue of a sad, emaciated, creepy-looking white guy bleeding and hanging on a cross. Church was not hard seats, long prayers and hours and hours of a man shouting about Hell and sin from a pulpit. Church was in a house in Houma.

Gamula's loving presence in that house made it my sacred temple. She was where I saw and experienced unconditional love. She was where I could be exactly who I was with no permission, apologies, requirements or expectations. I could do whatever I wanted, say whatever I wanted and feel whatever I wanted, and Gamula would still share her dessert with me. She was where I went when I was hurt, angry or sad. Her hugs and kisses consumed those feelings and I was once again wrapped in a space of total contentment; a space where nothing was missing; a space where I was happy.

Chapter 2

The Birth of Unworthiness

As I went on living and growing up, I eventually discovered why I had to go to church. I discovered why I had to suspend my play and pretend to want something I really didn't want. I discovered that when your grandmother dies, you no longer get something for nothing. You now have to earn kind words, smiles, warm hugs and dessert. Where before it was given freely, unconditional love—or at least the things I associated with it—now came with conditions. I had to do something or behave in a certain way to deserve to be in a space of contentment and happiness.

Eventually, I began to hear the words the preacher was shouting from the pulpit. I began to understand the words I was reading in the Bible during Sunday school. I began to cry with the people who were coming to church because they were lost and hopeless. In church, I discovered that I was one of the lost ones. There was something I was missing. I was missing God's love, not because He didn't want to love me but because my sinful nature was preventing it. I found out that I was unworthy of God's love because I was a sinner who deserved to die and face the worst kind of torture for all eternity.

This was shocking news! Gamula must not have known this. Thank God she never went to church or she would have discovered this about me. Because of her beauty, innocence and lack of information, she missed the evidence that proved I was an unworthy sinner.

Although, I can see how that was possible because I didn't even know; I apparently hid it from myself. As a child, lying on the ground with the sun on my face or sitting on the bank of the bayou looking at tadpoles in the shallow water, I didn't know I was unworthy. How would I know? I'd never seen, tasted or touched unworthiness. I could describe the soft, sand-papery feel of a dragonfly's wings or the silky squishiness of mud between my toes, but I could not describe unworthiness. I'd seen the sparkle of the bluest blue sky and I knew the feeling of cool water from the hose in contrast to the heat of the day. I knew those things. I'd experienced those things. I'd never experienced sin. What color was it? Did it grow in a garden? Did it fly, burrow in the ground or swim in the water? Could I feel it with my fingers or smell it from far away? Where was unworthiness and sin? I was unworthy of God's love but what did that mean?

While I saw no evidence of unworthiness it was

imperative that I believe it. Apparently there was a hole inside of me filled with sin. I was not an innocent little girl. I was really a fallen, filthy, evil, undeserving thing. It was this thing that twirled in a new Easter dress. It was this thing that sat in Gamula's lap and stole her affection. The fact that I didn't know or feel evil, sinful or unworthy meant nothing. The remedy for that ignorance was education.

I had to first know of and believe in my sinful nature in order to, then, be free of sin. I had to first be unworthy before I could be worthy. I had to first be missing something in order to see and believe that there was something better out there to get.

Chapter 3

Making What's Missing

If you have a complete puzzle, where no pieces are missing, why would you look for a missing piece? Why would you abandon the complete puzzle to go on a life-long journey to find what is not missing? You wouldn't. Only insanity would take that journey. Only insanity would fuel a search for what is not missing. As a child, I was a complete puzzle, a whole enigma, an undivided mystery. I wasn't missing anything so there was nothing more for me to get. This is what I knew and felt, but I had to believe something different from what I knew. I had to believe I was missing something. I had to believe that I was separate from God and I had to believe this in order to be made whole.

As I learned more and more about sin and my many deficiencies, I found there was a lot of value in the belief that I lack something. With belief in lack comes expectation, entitlement, excitement and the concept of "more". Belief in my unworthiness would allow me to get something; to get more. Believing I was a sinner was necessary.

The Hebrew word for sin is derived from an archery term that means "to miss the mark". In archery, if you miss the mark, you don't get the prize, so you must try again. "Miss" has two meanings: "the absence of something" or "to fail to hit a target or mark". Because I was complete and not missing or lacking anything, I had to make something to miss. First I had to make a mark so that I could, then, miss it.

But how can I take something that is whole and make it incomplete? I have to redefine it. I have to create my own definition of wholeness. So that's what I did. I redefined myself by adding my own knowledge to the complete puzzle that I am. The knowledge I added was the mark. My marks were concepts and beliefs that I was a girl, smart, funny, honest, obedient, courageous and spiritual. These were all terms that defined me, and each term had its opposite. These were all terms that everyone would agree with and support as absolutely true.

These marks and the many more that I made could come and go, giving the illusion that I was missing something. For example, telling a lie could very easily remove the mark of "honest". Judgment and evaluation added another dimension that ensured I could never hit the mark. All of this made sinning inevitable. Missing the mark, by either failing to hit it or by failing to have a mark in the first place, was guaranteed.

Adding my own knowledge and judgment was the process that I used to manufacture lack, create loss and make what was missing. In reality, there is no mark. A mark is a concept, a mental fabrication. At no time have the concepts of "woman", "spiritual" or "courageous" ever defined who I really am, but I needed to ignore this if I was going to be successful in becoming something "better" and getting more. Absolute belief in the marks I had made was the tool I needed to make what was missing real—the tool I needed to make concepts substantial, sure and undeniable. Belief in what I had made was what I needed to be a sinner.

So I began to believe, without question, what others were telling me about who I was and what I lacked. With each belief, I created myself; I created a self made of concepts. I believed it when I was told that I was a horrible sinner and unworthy of God's love. I also believed that I was a girl, and black, and skinny and funny and smart and tall and on and on and on. And I believed all of it while experience told me it was not the entire truth; it was not the whole story.

Believing allowed me to create borders around my wholeness... like pieces of a puzzle. With each belief I created more limits and more opportunities for lack. The more concepts and marks I made and believed in, the more opportunities I had to miss them. Missing them was evidence of my unworthiness and sinful nature. But this was a good thing because

I already believed that salvation was what I wanted and needed if I was going to be happy for eternity.

I needed to be unworthy before I could be saved. Unworthiness must come before salvation. While church sermons, others' opinions and others' stories were helpful in planting the seed of unworthiness in my mind, I was the one who nourished the seed. What was it without which the seed of unworthiness would not have sprouted? What was the fertile ground that allowed unworthiness to penetrate within the deepest recesses of my soul? It was my own thoughts.

Believing the voice in my head was the life-blood of the seed of unworthiness. Absolute belief in thoughts like, "you shouldn't have done that", "you were wrong", "you're not worthy", "you've failed again", "you never do anything right", "you don't deserve to be happy" and a thousand other statements allowed unworthiness to bloom in all its magnificence. Now, I knew it... I felt it... the evidence was all around me. I *was* unworthy. I *was* wrong. I was a sinner and I needed a savior.

Now I was grateful that I'd been made to attend church even when I didn't want to. I was grateful for the Bible, my minister, the authorities in my life, my thoughts, the Holy Spirit and all the other marks I had made and believed in. They all helped me discover my lack. As I lived my life, I missed the mark over and over and over again but I had a way out of the unworthiness and sin that I'd believed myself into.

Salvation was the key. Not only was salvation the key to eternal happiness, but with salvation came a whole host of benefits like God's favor, protection from my enemies, unexpected blessings, a personal relationship with Jesus, visits from the Holy Spirit, a personal prayer line to God, forgiveness if I missed any other marks, spiritual gifts and healing abilities—and this was just on Earth! After the bloody war of Armageddon, where I would be on the good side to witness the slaughter of Satan, his demons and all my earthly enemies (before they were all thrown into Hell forever), I would be gifted with a mansion, gold, a brand new earth and a problem-free eternal life. As far as I was concerned, unworthiness and a little earthly suffering was a small price to pay for all the rewards I was going to get.

The first step in getting all these treasures was admitting I was a sinner. I had to tell the truth about my sinful nature and ask God for forgiveness. So at the age of twelve I walked to the front of my church and sincerely asked Jesus to forgive me. With that confession and request for forgiveness, came tears of happiness, salvation, freedom from sin and hope for eternal life.

I'd found what was missing. I was no longer incomplete, I was whole again. I'd accepted Jesus into my heart and everything was now made right again. I was back in God's good graces. He would work on my behalf in the face of worldly problems. I was special. I was His, and as long as I obeyed Him, worshipped Him, acknowledged Him and put Him first in my life, I would be happy.

I understood that the occasional test would come to try my faith and allow me to prove that I was worthy of God's love, but even if I occasionally failed, I was still covered by His love so nothing could really harm me.

Not only had I been made complete, but I'd succeeded in making myself; a self that was capable of being incomplete and separate from God. I'd succeeded in making marks and successfully missing them. Salvation was proof that I had succeeded. Salvation is not needed if there's no sin. Salvation is only necessary if I've separated myself from God.

Eventually I grew to see salvation for what it really was; just another mark that I'd made and believed to be the absolute truth. Belief in salvation was planted alongside a very healthy, deep-rooted, robust belief in my unworthiness. The belief that I was unworthy was still there, still thriving and being watered and nourished every day. The horrible emotions that supported my thoughts of unworthiness were also still there.

The belief that I was saved, free from sin, and known and loved by God did not uproot this much stronger belief in unworthiness. If I could just uproot the belief in unworthiness and replace it with a different belief, everything would be fine. I would finally feel special, set apart and known by God. My thoughts would now be positive, uplifting and holy.

My emotions would support these thoughts and happiness would overshadow sadness, depression, anger and hopelessness.

But how could I uproot the powerful belief in unworthiness when the evidence that I was unworthy was all around me? It couldn't be denied. The proof was the fact that my life was filled with problems; problems in my relationships, financial problems, problems with negative thoughts, depression, low self-esteem, and terribly painful emotions. I was still missing marks. Marks like "you're smart", "you're honest", "you're courageous", "you're happy", "you're successful", "you're healthy", "you're spiritual" and "you're kind", were constantly being missed. At no time was I consistently any of these things. Much of the time I was none of these things. I was a horrible person, unworthy of God's love. I was still undeserving, full of sin and constantly seeking forgiveness of wrongdoing.

My inability to be what I thought I should be, or have what I thought I should have, was a problem. Constantly missing these and a plethora of other marks, was problematic and caused feelings of dissatisfaction, depression, anger and hopelessness; the same feelings that indicated I was not whole.

I was confused. Where was God? Wasn't he supposed to step in and help me make my life at least a little better on this earth? Wasn't salvation supposed to take away the marks and the resulting sin and make me whole again, clean again and "a new creature in Christ"? Wasn't salvation supposed to make it all better or at least lessen the pain? If so, it wasn't working. The same painful emotions, suffering and problems were still there—but this was my fault. I'd failed to remember that the marks I'd made were not real. They were simply mental constructs and judgments I'd created to re-define myself.

Luckily, belief is also just another concept. Because belief is not real, I could very easily drop one belief for another, and that's what I did. Where problems, suffering, pain and anguish were previously proof of my unworthiness, now the exact same problems, suffering, pain and anguish were proof of my salvation. I had to suffer. I had to sacrifice. I had to lose the things I loved most in the world. Salvation required it. I had to endure physical and emotional pain, and watch my enemies prosper while my world fell apart. That was the price of eternal life.

Instead of suffering and lack being the natural *result* of sinful behavior, now God *allowed* suffering to cleanse me, help me learn lessons, become better, more righteous, closer and more dependent on Him. A change in belief was all it took. Now my life would get better.

Chapter 4

A Leap of Doubt

After years of behaving and thinking in the way a Christian should behave and think, I began to question the lack of distinction between the life of the unworthy and unsaved and the life of the worthy and saved.

Something wasn't right. I had begun to love church and genuinely enjoy singing in the choir, reading my Bible and witnessing to others, but it wasn't making much difference in my life. Although my behaviors (most of the time) lined up with the directives in the Bible and I felt like I had a relationship with God, I wasn't fulfilled or happy.

Shouldn't there be a noted difference between the life of the sinner and the life of the saved other than behaviors (although some of the "saved" could easily be mistaken for "sinners" and vice versa)? Shouldn't I feel better, happier, and more joyful now, after salvation?

Even as a Christian, I found myself constantly

looking in the future for happiness. I was very rarely happy *now*, something was always missing, there was always something more that I wanted and nothing was ever as it should be. Even as a Christian, worry, regret, fear and uncertainty were my constant companions, which meant I had to rely on hope, faith and trust to get me through the day.

Every gospel song I heard and sang in the choir was about hope that things would get better, faith that God would intervene on my behalf and trust that everything would be okay tomorrow. At some point, I got tired of waiting for tomorrow. Tomorrow never came for me or anyone else. Never being satisfied and waiting for something more and better became my life. Satisfaction and happiness in the present moment, regardless of what was occurring, was extremely rare.

Living in constant states of disquiet, ungratefulness, unhappiness and dissatisfaction is no way to live, and I didn't want to live like that anymore. I didn't want to have hope or faith that life would get better "tomorrow", or when Jesus came back, or when I died and went to heaven. I didn't want to have faith and trust in a better future or a different outcome.

I wanted to be happy *now*. I wanted peace *now*. But I couldn't just be peaceful or stop being dissatisfied. Peace and satisfaction relied on a certain set of conditions; conditions that were not being met in my life.

I didn't want to give up my belief in salvation because I still wanted eternal life and all the stuff that came along with being on the good side, so I thought that maybe if I sacrificed more, prayed more, attended church more, tithed more, repented more, helped others more, fasted more... maybe if I did all these things and more, the suffering, pain and depression would subside. I'd feel better about myself and God would be happy with me and give me something for doing all these wonderful things.

So I switched churches, I began to tithe more, I fasted more, I volunteered more, I prayed more, I read my Bible more and I was sure to repent for every little thought I judged to be out of line with God's Word.

It didn't work. I tried it all and it didn't work. I was still miserable.

Maybe I didn't try hard enough. Maybe I needed another pastor, another church, a different husband, a different job, a better image of myself, more obedient children, a happier disposition, a healthier body, a more positive attitude, more sincerity, a better relationship with Jesus, more compassion, more courage or less pride. Maybe I needed to make better choices. Maybe I needed to wait a little longer for God to come through for me. Maybe I needed a different mark; a better mark. Maybe I just hadn't learned my life lesson and problems were just opportunities for me to be more holy, saved, spiritual and dependent of God.

That's right! I was *supposed* to suffer and have problems. This was the price, the sacrifice I had to make to be worthy of God's love. Jesus suffered so I had to suffer. I made a bad decision, not God. I was disobedient, not God. I couldn't blame God. This was entirely my fault. He was innocent and only wished to love me. I just had to be patient, pray and wait on Him. He didn't have to do anything for me if He didn't want to. I didn't deserve His love at all. Suffering, problems and sacrifice were a small price to pay for what He had already done for me. I sang this song for years. I made excuse after excuse for this God and His inability to keep his promises. Blaming God for anything was not an option. So I remained on my quest to get more.

I had lots of ideas on how I should be better and how I should view suffering and problems and I tried all of them, but I was not satisfied with the results. The result was still misery and unhappiness and a continuation of the tireless and never-ending search for something better. Salvation didn't work. Saved from what? Hell? The story of Hell is a child's fairy-tale when you're living the reality. When you're in a fetal position on the floor, thinking of ways you can end your life, and crying until you can't breathe, while physically feeling the tightness of despair and hopelessness gripping every cell in your body... the story of Hell means absolutely nothing. I didn't need a Devil or fire and brimstone as punishment for being a sinner. My own thoughts and emotions were the fire and brimstone. My own hopelessness, helplessness and failure at life were punishment enough. An outside agent was not necessary.

Belief in salvation and unworthiness were beliefs in nothing because that's what they provided me; absolutely nothing.

I'd made a mistake. I'd mistakenly thought that all the work I'd put into limiting and redefining myself would result in a reward, a boon, a better outcome. Belief in unworthiness and subsequent salvation was supposed to get me something more; something better than what I had before. It didn't. Now I was trapped by what I'd made. I was trapped by my own definition of myself. I was confined in all the concepts and beliefs in my mind. I was at the mercy of the marks I'd made.

I was a 34-year-old unhappy African American woman, mother, sister and wife with no self-esteem and a laundry list of problems. This is how I had redefined myself. I was a person in search of something more. And I was right about this. No one would argue with my definition of myself. This is who I was. While there were moments of happiness, joy, contentment, laughter and beauty they never lasted. Happiness was fleeting and dissatisfaction always overcame contentment. Time always passed and life always ended so I was continually searching.

I was exhausted. I didn't want to do this anymore. Praying, trusting, waiting and worrying is hard work. I was imprisoned by the incessant chatter in my head and all my static beliefs. I wanted out but I didn't know how to escape the prison that I had made. At the same time, I wanted to keep this prison, because I made it.

Knowledge gave me the power to redefine myself and control my life. Redefining myself made me a creator. A creator is a thing or person who brings something into existence. Using knowledge, judgment and belief I made myself, other people and circumstances. I literally made the world. I believed the world was or should be a certain way and my judgments made it the way I wanted it to be.

When it came to other people, they had to either agree with my version of the world or they had to suffer for failing to agree. Those who didn't agree were my enemies and would eventually be taken care of by my vengeful yet merciful God; whom I had made and who was, of course, on my side. In addition to creation I also had the power to judge and forgive others. When someone I'd judged as an enemy affronted my version of the world, it was my prerogative to forgive or not.

Because I had the power to create, judge and forgive, I was on the throne. I was Creator. *I* was God, not the "God" of the Bible. It was my belief in the God of the Bible... not His reality, which gave Him life. The God of the Bible has no reality without my belief. God is a mark, just like every other mark that I'd made. In fact, God was the culmination of all the marks I'd made. God could be snuffed out and forgotten in less than a second if I chose not to believe in Him. I had the power... not this God that I chose to believe in. I enjoyed this power. I liked it. I liked it a lot.

But reigning over a world is thirsty work. The endless judging, evaluating, believing and decision making is exhausting. Being God is hard work, especially when it requires believing something completely contrary to the obvious. Believing in what I'd made required a lot of effort. I carried beliefs around with me the way Atlas, the mythological Titan, carried the world on his shoulders. I carried them around for so long I didn't notice the weight until they were gone.

Chapter 5

Firing God

One day after arriving home and opening my mail to see a foreclosure notice, countless bills, a summons to appear in court and several other pieces of unpleasant correspondence, I went to sit on my bed defeated, depressed and hopeless. I'd been attempting to find a church for months so I could, once again, try to find some relief from my world of problems. It appeared as if I'd need to double my efforts.

My life was a mess and I needed God in the worst way. There was a book on my dresser that I'd gotten from a minister I'd met a few weeks before. He suggested I read it to gather encouragement, hope and help to "stay strong" and wait for God to intervene in my life. I'd put off reading it because I was either too busy or too tired. In that moment of total hopelessness, I reached for the book as if I were a drowning man reaching upward toward a hand in the water in a final attempt to save his own life. I needed to hear a story of how someone else had survived another day.

I needed to read the story of how a woman who was just as hopeless and depressed as I, was able to meet her challenges and come through victorious.

Until I had my own story to tell, I had to depend on the suffering and triumph of strangers to help me take my next breath. I picked up the book and began to read. I don't remember the title of the book or what specifically it was about, but I do remember reading something that frightened me. It was something about the requirement to remove evil spirits from your house in order to invite God in. Growing up Christian, this was not a new concept to me and I'd heard it before, but for some reason, reading this really scared me. The fear was followed by a burst of anger.

Here I was once again, going to God for help and all I get is fear and "you're not good enough yet". This is all I'd ever gotten. It's always been "Cheryl, not yet", "Cheryl, just wait" or "Cheryl, be patient, there's more that you have to do". I was sick of it. I threw the book to the floor, placed my head in my hands and thought, "I can't do this anymore", "this can't be right", "this can't be what life is about". Then I lifted my head and said with all the feeling and heart I could muster:

God, I'm tired of being afraid of you. I'm tired of having to meet certain conditions in order for you to help me. I'm tired of you breaking your promises and I refuse to continue to make excuses for you. I'm no longer depending on you to make my life better. You have done absolutely nothing for me and I am no better off than the "sinner". God, I don't love you, I don't trust you and I don't believe you. You're a liar and a fraud and you're no better than I am. God, you can fuck off. You're fired!

Immediately after I told God to fuck off, something happened. While there was a tiny twinge of disbelief in what I'd just done and a little fear that something tragic would befall me, there was also a profound feeling of freedom. I felt like I'd been released from shackles. It was because I was finally honest with myself. I told the truth. I'd been pretending to know, love and trust in a God that I really did not know, love or trust.

My motivation to love was born out of fear of current and future punishment and anticipation of a future reward. Loving God was only ever about what I could and would get. I wanted to be on the "right" side because I was going to get something for that—eternal life. Why in the world would I suffer, sacrifice, pray or tithe if I wasn't going to get something for that? I wouldn't—no one would. God was a meal ticket; a bridge to something better.

With my declaration, I gave that up. I relinquished my meal ticket for something else. What that something else was, I didn't know.

I call this my prodigal moment. It was the moment I came to my senses. In the Bible story of the prodigal son it was the father who ran to his son once the son decided to turn around. By turning away from my own judgments, knowledge and understanding, heaven was now rushing towards me to welcome me back to the place that I had never left... but I didn't realize it at the time.

As far as I knew, I was no longer on the right side. I'd turned my back on God. I'd relinquished my throne and turned away from my knowledge. I'd given up the promise of eternal life. By turning away from the God that was created out of my judgments, knowledge and belief, I automatically turned toward what I thought was the unknown.

But if I could not go to God, then where could I go for protection from this world? Where could I go to find happiness? I had no idea what to do. I'd gone from an unquestioned belief in God to total and complete doubt. I was afraid. The God that I'd known from childhood was my anchor. That God was where I went for comfort. Even though the good things were few and far between, I'd believed that anything good in my life *was* because of the God made of concepts and beliefs. It had to be, everything I touched turned to crap so there had to be a God who was causing good things to happen.

Maybe I'd made a mistake. Maybe I should recant what I'd said and apologize. He'd forgive me. That's what He does. He'd take me back. He'd done it before. Maybe this is just another test for a lesson I must learn. Maybe this is just another hurdle I must get over. I considered it for a moment, but I knew I couldn't go back. Everything I'd said was true. If I went back, I'd be going back to a *hope* of God and a *belief* in a Savior. I was done hoping and believing so going back was not an option because there was nothing to go back to.

Even though I'd given God the boot, I knew there was something going on here that was "bigger" than me. Somehow I knew it... I could feel it. But what was it? I had to find out and I had to find it on my own terms. I was no longer relying on church sermons, bibles, seminars, songs, college courses, conversations with others and other people's experiences to tell me about God. I was no longer relying on what I knew and understood. But how in the world could I discover something without reading about it, asking other people or believing what I'd been taught?

Something very interesting happened almost immediately after my little talk with God. I felt the strongest compulsion to read the Bible story of Adam and Eve. I did not hear a voice or see writing on the wall or anything weird like that, I actually felt this compulsion. It wasn't a thought in my head, but a full-body directive to read that story. Of course I resisted. Why would I read the Bible when I just vowed to never again have anything to do with books and other people's interpretations? I resisted this compulsion for a few days but it became so bothersome that I had to finally read the damned story. I read it.

Nothing profound happened but I did begin to question the story. I remember calling my two older sisters, who are very well-versed in the Bible, and asking them what they thought about the story. I questioned why there were two stories. I wanted to know why God had to make Adam from dirt when in the previous story he only spoke the word and man and woman were created. I wanted to know more about the Tree of the Knowledge of Good and Evil. Why was it there? Why give man a choice on whether or not he wanted knowledge?

These questions led to more questions, which led to more questions. I was quite excited because I felt like something new was opening up for me. I'd never considered questioning what I knew. Why would I question what I already know and have evidence of? Why indeed?

Chapter 6

The Release from Fear

I am deathly afraid of caterpillars. I will gladly wrap a snake around my body five times and kiss it on the mouth, but if a caterpillar falls on my blouse or wriggles across my path, you're going to have to call the paramedics. Do you know why? It's because caterpillars make nests in pecan trees. I grew up on a plantation called Pecan Grove; a plantation with a plethora of pecan trees. You'd think growing up with a thing would cause you to get used to it and maybe even enjoy it. Not so. I am terrified of caterpillars. In the spring and summer, caterpillars rained from the sky and I could hear them hit the hot, floury Louisiana dirt like fat, hairy, horned, droplets of wiggly grossness.

Caterpillars are a cake-walk compared to the terror and fear I felt as I began to discover who God really is, because discovering who I really am happened simultaneously. Discovery did not involve learning something new; discovery involved unlearning what

I thought I knew. Discovery was looking at my judgments and questioning the absolute truth of them. Discovery was dropping my beliefs for no beliefs at all.

A few months after the incident in the bedroom and well into my questioning of all I thought I knew about myself and God, there was an experience that totally changed the game. While the bedroom experience caused me to turn away from what I knew, this experience had me in a dead run... desperate to find the home I believed I'd lost. I was sitting at work one early morning checking my emails. I'd been sitting there for about an hour when suddenly, and for no obvious reason at all, I became terrified. My heart began beating very fast, and I broke into a cold sweat. Horrific chills went up and down my spine as I slowly looked at my body and all around me wondering what was going on.

I lifted my shaking hands, looked at my suddenly sweaty palms and thought, *Why is this happening?* Nothing was going on around me so why was I experiencing bone-chilling terror? Was I having a heart attack? But that was ridiculous! I was a healthy young woman with no major health problems. But obviously something was happening. Was I dying? *Oh my God*, I thought, *I'm dying!*

With that thought, I knew it was true. I was dying. Through my fear, panic and confusion I knew that I was about to die and there was nothing I could do about it but accept the inevitable. My last thought before I died was, *What will happen to my babies?* Prepared to let go of this life, I calmly accepted the fact that my life was ending right there, in my chair, at work. With my life still in a shambles, without having accomplished all I wanted to accomplish, without saying goodbye to all the people I loved, without hugging and kissing my children one last time; I was leaving this life unfinished and incomplete and I was powerless to change it.

Right then, the terror quickly dissipated and transitioned into something very different: I suddenly felt as if I was in "Eternity". A rush of waves and waves of what I can only refer to as "Eternity" were in me and all around me. I was these waves of Eternity. Not only was I in Eternity (as opposed to being in time), but my computer, my desk, the floor, the ceiling, my phone, my pens and pencils, the wall, my cell phone and the sound of my heater were in Eternity with me. As I looked at my computer, I thought, *What is a computer doing here?* I was curious about there being a computer. The computer wasn't wrong, it was interesting. It was interesting because I knew it was not a computer. I didn't know what it was, but I did know what it wasn't. It was clearly not a computer.

This was the case for everything around me, including me. I didn't know what I was, but I did know what I was not. I was not a Cheryl, a woman, African American, smart, pretty or any of the other labels I'd placed on myself. I did not know what I was, and there was no desire or need to know. Even though I was seeing what appeared to be an office and objects, the experience of *this is not what you think it is* trumped everything I saw. The thought, *I'm already here,* arose in my mind but I knew, even before the thought, that it was true. I was already in Eternity and "I" was not Cheryl or the appearances around her. There was also a strong feeling of there being nothing to do and no reason for anything. Whatever was done was already done, and anything I was doing was unnecessary.

This amazing experience didn't seem to last very long but it totally changed the trajectory of my search. Now other questions arose like, *How can I be in eternity if I'm (1) alive, (2) at work, (3) imperfect and (4) in a shitty place in my life?* I'd told God to fuck off about two months ago, I didn't like my husband, I hated myself, and I was sure I was ruining the future happiness of my children because I couldn't get my act together. I was not worthy enough to be in Eternity. I didn't deserve such peace; at least not yet.

I had to be cleansed, perfected, forgiven and judged as worthy before I made it to Heaven. Everybody knew this. I had to do something or improve myself to accomplish eternal peace and freedom; this was also common knowledge. I had to sacrifice, admit my unworthiness, seek forgiveness and obey spiritual rules to experience this unconditional love. I had to work my way from brokenness to wholeness. Isn't that the way it's supposed to be? Isn't that what the Bible says?

In that moment, I saw that Life is not interested in what the Bible says nor does it care about what is "supposed" to be. My ideas about the way things should be mean nothing and have absolutely nothing to do with reality. This experience reminded me of what I already knew; what I knew as a little girl standing in the rain in my grandfather's yard in Louisiana. I am already whole. I am already worthy. I am already unconditionally loved. I am not missing anything. There is no reason to search for more; there is no more. Searching for what I am not missing is me creating my own personal Hell. Creation is a done deal and nothing else need be nor can be added. I did not see this experience as my moment of awakening or enlightenment; at the time I was not familiar with those terms anyway. I only saw this as a reminder. It was a gentle reminder that I was doing too much. I was working and striving for something that I already had... that I already was... eternal life. There was nothing more to get.

After this amazing, peaceful, divine occurrence, my life went to Hell in a hand basket. Problems exploded and lit up the sky like the fourth of July. My marriage got even worse, the police were constantly at my house, I was arrested and placed in detention, I lost my home, I lost all my possessions, my paycheck was garnished by two different creditors, my car was repossessed, my children were displaced, I was totally embarrassed, disappointed in myself, extremely depressed, fully dependent on the kindness of my family and more hopeless than I'd ever been before. I felt abandoned, lost and wholly confused.

My primary thought was, there is no way the experience I had was real. I cannot be Eternal Life. What I'm experiencing now, is not what Heaven is "supposed" to be. Maybe that experience was a taste of what will happen in the future after I get my act together. Maybe it was just to encourage me to hold on a little while longer because peace and joy are right around the corner. But I knew that wasn't true. I knew I was Home right now.

As time went by, I began to have other experiences that resulted in the continued questioning of what I thought I knew about myself and this world. Some of them filled me with terror, while others were more subtle reminders.

For instance, one beautiful and bright spring day I was driving to the grocery store when suddenly I went blind. I could see the road, the sky, my steering wheel and everything around me, but I felt as if I were blind. It felt like I had walked into a pitch black room, and I was reflexively opening my eyes wide in an attempt to see in the darkness; which is what most of us do when we walk into a dark room. While driving, I was "seeing" in complete and total darkness.

There was another incident, again while I was driving, where I felt what I can only describe as a "cork" being placed in my head that prevented me from thinking. This "cork" blocked the movement of thought. I was driving, turning right or left when

I needed to, but I was unable to think about it or anything else. At first it was shocking and a little interesting but I quickly became extremely frightened. Because I couldn't think I felt like someone had placed me in chains. Without the movement of thought, I felt like I was imprisoned. I then began to panic but before I could pull over to the side of the road the "cork" was removed and thoughts came back. This was a huge relief and I no longer felt imprisoned. I was now able to think about turning left or right or what I was going to have for dinner that night.

These experiences and many others only generated more questions and doubt about what I thought I knew until the truth became undeniable. The truth was I didn't know anything, including the belief that there was an "I" who could know. The truth was, every judgment I'd ever made and believed in was not true. The truth was, belief is unnecessary because you don't need to believe what is real and present now; and what is real and present now is all there is. The experience I had at work is no different than any other experience. It came and went, but it did get my attention like no other experience had before. It's this attention that I've come to notice more and more. The attention is always there, ever-present, with no past and no future.

There are countless names for this but I like to refer to it as the Present. The Present does not need to be believed in or hoped for. I don't need faith in it and I don't need to wait for it. This present moment is not missing nor is it missing anything. You don't need to read about it, ask someone's opinion or meditate to get there. No one has to sacrifice themselves or die to obtain the Present. I don't have to go through someone in order to get to this Present moment. It's all here... simple and ordinary, and it does not belong to anyone. No one owns the Present; and attempts to redefine it with judgments, knowledge, thoughts, opinions, interpretations, beliefs or religious frameworks only cause untold suffering and pointless searching.

The Present can only be what it is—this plain, ordinary moment. I never added to it. The judgments, marks and concepts I made and believed in never changed the Present. I never created something different than what was already here. I never chose something other than what was already here; choosing to see that I never made that choice, released me from a prison that I was never in.

Seeing that all there is is this present moment reminded me of a scene in *Indiana Jones and the Last Crusade*. Indiana Jones (played by Harrison Ford) had to choose the true Holy Grail from an altar of assorted cups. Drinking from the actual Holy Grail (the cup from which Jesus drank at the Last Supper) would grant eternal life to the drinker, while drinking from the wrong chalice would immediately kill him. The character who chose before Indiana selected a golden chalice beautifully set with diamonds and other jewels. Before drinking from the cup he described it as a cup fit for the "king of kings". When he drank from this false grail, he rapidly aged within seconds and died. Indiana, however, bypassed all the golden, embellished, beautifully jewel-encrusted cups and realized that the most modest, unassuming, simple and ordinary cup was that of the carpenter Jesus.

That is what I am trying to convey here. The simple truth is ordinary, open, and shared by all. No one "has it" and it is not reserved for a select few with special connections to various saints. Truth does not need to be attained and behavior has nothing whatsoever to do with it. Truth needs no defense nor armies of "believers" to fight for it. It doesn't need to be embellished with experiences, stories of suffering, Heaven, eternity or Hell. Truth simply is, and it cannot be known because there is nothing or no one separate from it to know it.

What I have said here cannot be believed. I am not an enlightened being who knows something that no one else knows. I have not changed religions or swapped one set of beliefs for another. I have not gone from one level of consciousness to another. I've simply placed my judgments and beliefs on trial, questioned them and found them to be untrue. I see that I am not who I thought and believed I was. I see that there is nothing behind, underneath, or above what I'm experiencing. It's all right here. Sacrifice and suffering is not required to "reach" what is already present.

Whatever is, is all there is which is this... whatever this is. I can't know what it is because I am what it is... whatever it is. Knowing what it is or who I am, is not possible nor is it necessary. All I need do is see, and seeing happens naturally, without my interference.

Nothing that I know is true. That's it. If you feel like this moment is not enough, there must be more to get, or there has to be something better, then you're searching for what is not missing. You're looking *for* the promise of eternal life *from* Eternity. Call off the search. We're already Home.

I never did improve, change or transform myself. My plan to solve my problems never panned out. As I write this, I still don't have a car, I'm still knee deep in debt, my children are still displaced, my home is still in foreclosure and my marriage is still on a steaming pile of rubbish headed for the garbage heap; at least that's the story. But as the author of this story, I don't mind. The story can be whatever it is, and while it will eventually change, I will not. I never did find the happiness I was looking for. I never got a chance to make my life work and arrange all the pieces exactly the way I wanted them to be. I was mistaken about everything. There is nothing more to get. In Reality, this is it; which is much more than I could have ever hoped for.

PART 2

BY THE WAY

Understanding, then seeing that *this is it* was a very complicated, frustrating and frightening process; and it isn't over. I learn and see something new almost every day. Each day is like an exciting and fascinating magic show—full of surprises and wonder. How can something so simple be so wondrous? My own knowledge served only to dull, muddle and mute my full capacity and freedom.

Questioning my thoughts and beliefs and using my own experience cleared the fog of what I thought was absolute truth. Acknowledging that I did not have the market cornered on truth (no one does) brought clarity and a gradual shining away of the dullness.

However, there were four core concepts that I really struggled with: sin, responsibility, belief and perfection. My belief in these concepts as absolute truths was very hard to question because they were the cornerstone of my belief in unworthiness and salvation. While interpretation is neither right nor wrong, interpretation or perception that was "closer" to my present experience seemed to resonate more for me.

Sin

Sin is commonly seen as an immoral act or a transgression against divine law. In church, I would commonly hear that someone was "caught up in her sin" or "trapped in his sin". It seemed as if we are like spiders and "sin" was the intricate and complicated pattern we wove. But spiders do not get caught in their own webs. Yes, they weave amazingly intricate and complicated patterns but they never get caught or imprisoned in what they make; and neither do we.

I believed that humanity's sinful nature was born out of Adam and Eve's disobedience and poor decision-making. Adam and Eve have been blamed for thousands of years for our innate penchant to sin and disobey God. Most of us know the Bible story of Adam and Eve. If you don't, the gist of the story is that God gave Adam a directive to refrain from eating the fruit of the Tree of Knowledge of Good and Evil; the forbidden fruit. Adam, at some point, communicated this to Eve. Eve, being enticed and lied to by the serpent, disobeyed God and Adam and ate the fruit anyway. Not only did she eat the fruit, she offered it to Adam and he ate of the fruit as well.

God, while walking in the Garden of Eden, confronted Adam, discovered the couple's disobedience and banished them from the Garden to earn their living "by the sweat of their brow". He also punished the serpent for tempting Eve to disobey His directive. This "original sin" of disobedience and failure to hit the mark, standard or law that had been set by God caused the downfall of all mankind.

This sin also made Jesus necessary as the "perfect sacrifice" to take on the sins of the world. Because Jesus never sinned, or never missed the mark set by God, he was an example to us that it is possible not to sin. Sacrificing a perfect—in other words 'sinless'—son of God made it possible for us to return to paradise and be with God for eternal life.

Using present experience instead of taking words, context or religions frameworks as the "gospel truth", I began to question this concept of sin. What is sin? What if sin is simply our interpretation and judgment of what is? Consider for one moment the possibility that sin is not wrong or evil. What if sinning and judgment are completely involuntary? In other words, sin is not a decision or a choice.

Sin is akin to learning. Learning happens naturally. For instance, we don't have to go to school to know not to put our hand in a fire. The first time it happens there is a reaction that the body learns and so automatically avoids fire from that point on. Newborn babies learn to breathe, blink and cry. They're not conscious happenings but more of an impulse or reflex that the body learns and that from then on happens by itself. Eating the fruit of the Tree of the Knowledge of Good and Evil simply means we are constantly seeking to know or learn. This attempt or impulse to "know" is sin.

Attempting to know is to attempt to be like God, who is all-knowing. This does not mean that God is an entity, person or thing that knows: it means "He" is made of Knowing or Intelligence; He is All-Knowing. Because God is not a concept and cannot be known or judged, it appears as if our attempt or impulse to know and judge has caused God to banish us from the Garden of Eden. Knowing who God is (which is impossible) seems to separate us from Him because you must first be separate from something to know it.

If you believe you're a person, reading words in a book, then you are eating of fruit of the Tree of Knowledge of Good and Evil. You are making and believing in marks and concepts that you've made. You know and judge; therefore you are sinning by attempting to be like God.

But keep in mind that sin has *nothing to do* with behavior. Sin happens before behavior. Knowledge and judgment happen in the mind and have *nothing* to do with behavior, and *everything* to do with your mind. Behavior is a non-issue when it comes to sin. Sin is not good or bad. It isn't evil or wicked. It's simply an attempt to know. What we must understand is that Truth is not a thing that can be known, captured, described and judged, and Truth has nothing to do with behavior either. They are both in the mind. In our minds, we sin, when we attempt to capture truth with our own knowledge. I say "attempt" because at no time have we ever been successful in capturing and owning Truth.

We were never banished from the Garden of Eden. We willingly left. The Garden of Eden is right now. We are currently in a space where we have everything we need. We choose to leave when we believe in what we've learned. Believing our own knowledge and judgment gives us control and we like control. We like what we've made, but at some point we cease to ignore the obvious fact that we really know nothing.

To say that Jesus did not sin only means that he saw this. Jesus—and many others before and after him—saw the war is not between flesh and blood, but in your mind. Not your mind and another mind; just yours. This is not seen with human eyes or with a human brain but with a different kind of vision; the same vision that we all have but have chosen to ignore in order to preserve our illusion of control. The concept of sin is not true. Any interpretation is not true and this is also seen... eventually.

Chapter 2

Responsibility

"**Y**ou can't blame God for your problems. *You* made the wrong choice, not God." This is what I would hear often from my family when discussing a problem I had or when voicing a frustration with God or with a scripture in the Bible. They were right. It was my responsibility. It is always and only ever my responsibility.

Typically God is only responsible if He "allowed" something to happen, and even then regardless of how heinous, bloody or evil the deed is... it was "for my own good and for God's glory". But before I'd take full blame there were always plenty of others to blame for my problems. These were my enemies. I needed my enemies. Enemies were critical in my quest to always be on the "right" side and they were integral in my need to shift the blame.

In the Christian faith, our primary enemy is Satan or the Devil. According to the story, Satan was once one of God's highest Angels. He was the most beautiful and powerful, but because he wanted to be like God, he was cast out of Heaven. Satan, Adam and Eve were all cast out for the very same reason. As a child of God, Satan was always the culprit behind my problems. He got a lot of credit for manipulating people, objects, feelings, emotions, weather, thinking and circumstances to specifically target us: the children of God. Life was the orchestra and Satan was the conductor who would look to God for His approval to wreak havoc and create catastrophe. God may have gotten a pass but Satan was the go-to guy as the primary enemy held responsible, not only for my problems, but the problems in the world.

Whether we believe in Satan or not, we all have enemies and others to blame. If the goal is happiness, our enemies are legion. These enemies or obstacles to our happiness are family members, friends, acquaintances, strangers, spouses and people who perpetrate situations that result in an unhealthy and immoral society, a corrupt political climate, ungodly religious institutions, hostile workplaces, unjust laws, senseless wars, rampant famine, uninhibited destruction of the natural environment, animal cruelty and genocide. We often see nature as our enemy, too, when she brings about disease, famine and natural disasters. We have no control over other people and we certainly have no control over nature, so why not place blame where blame belongs?

Most times we may see ourselves as innocent bystanders—only seeking to live a good life and protect ourselves and the ones we love from our enemies. So we build strong houses, we get good jobs, we collect close friends, we join movements, we become advocates, we accumulate knowledge, we seek divine help through an organized religion or some form of spirituality, and we evaluate and judge to ensure we are always on the "right" side. With these protections in place our enemies remain outside of us, contained and as far away as possible.

Can we really blame our enemies for our unhappiness? Are they responsible? What makes an enemy an enemy? Someone is only my enemy if I judge them as such. A person, situation or circumstance is only an enemy if you say so. Someone else may not see them as an enemy but as a wonderful and loyal friend, so it's your judgment and evaluation that makes them an enemy; not their behavior. Who's responsible for your judgment? You are. I am responsible for the judgments I make and you are always responsible for the judgments you make. If you judge something as wrong, evil, sinful or wicked you are responsible for that judgment, not the person or thing that you are judging. Likewise, judging something as good is your responsibility as well.

Responsibility and judgment rise together; there can't be one without the other. All day long we try to place responsibility for our judgments on something outside of us. This is like believing blooming flowers are responsible for sunshine, or the rising tide causes a full moon. Your judgment happens before the concept of "enemy". My judgment happens before the concept of "problems". Our judgment happens before the concept of "evil". Enemies, problems and evil don't *cause* judgment. It's the other way around. Our judgment is the cause. You are responsible for enemies, problems and evil.

It seems easier to simply blame and punish others for our judgments, and this we do on a large scale in the cases of the holocaust and Rwandan genocide or on a seemingly smaller scale like a disagreement between two people. We can certainly continue to hold others responsible for our judgments but we can decide to choose another alternative. We can decide to accept responsibility for our judgments. We don't have to punish ourselves for our judgments, just see that we are judging and take responsibility for it.

My family is right. I cannot blame God, but neither can I blame Satan, demons, politicians, laws, the government, nature or religion. It's my judgment that is the cause. I am responsible. It is not demonic forces, generational curses or your enemies that are preventing you from being happy and peaceful—it's you. You are the cause and demonic forces are the effect. I am the cause and enemies are the effect. This "you" that is made of judgments, concepts and beliefs is the only seeming obstacle that need be recognized... not overcome, simply looked at and seen for what it is—a simple error; an untrue judgment.

Like sin, judgment happens in the mind and you can look around you and see the effects of your thinking. Notice your thoughts and judgments and witness what you have created. Look at all the concepts and labels around you. The world is not your enemy; you are. Judgment is not evil, wicked, wrong or an abomination; nor is it right, good or holy—it's simply unnecessary. There is no need for it. Whatever is here is here before and without your judgment of it. There is no opposition here, unless that is what you want. You are responsible for your judgments. I am responsible for my judgments. There's no one else to blame.

Chapter 3
Belief

What do we mean when we declare we do not believe in something? Most times it means we have not experienced that particular thing so we imagine or create an idea of it. We create a mental construct or concept that we then believe in the absence of the real thing. We have no evidence to support a belief other than imagination and judgment.

First, belief is always about what is not present. There is no need to believe in what is present because what is present is here, real and directly experienced. You can only believe in what is not present. Second, belief is always about uncertainty—in fact, you can replace the word "belief" with the word "uncertain". "I believe in unicorns" is the same as "I am uncertain of the existence of unicorns". "I do not believe in unicorns" is the same as "I am uncertain of the existence of unicorns".

Both declarations mean the same thing. Why? Because we only believe when we don't know... we only believe when we're uncertain, and the only thing we can ever be certain of is this present moment; and again, this present moment does not require belief. Anything other than this present moment is a belief, a story, a judgment, imagination and uncertainty. Belief keeps us living in uncertainty and out of the present. Belief removes us from what is here now.

"God", "All-Knowing", the "Present" is what is here now, but we don't want this. We want more. So we choose to leave the Garden of Eden, in search of more. As long as we want more, we willingly and with our full consent remove ourselves out of the clear, unambiguous, factual, certainty of the Present moment. The Present is all that is ever known. It is the only thing that is real. What is real does not need a cause. What is real is here before sin, belief and judgment. Sin, belief and judgment need something to be here first before they can arise. Like sin and judgment, belief is in the mind and is also unnecessary because there is no more to get.

There is nothing that is not present. There is nothing missing or hidden from you. I thought there was so I had to believe until it arrived. I see now that this was all wasted effort. There is nothing right or wrong with belief, it's just not needed.

Perfection

"So be perfect, just as your heavenly Father is perfect." This is a well-known saying of Jesus and one that all Christians hope to live up to. Perfection is the goal with Heaven as the reward. But what did Jesus mean when he said this? I have no idea, but the common thinking is he's directing us to strive towards a life without sin. But what if this means something else?

Let's consider another interpretation for a moment. Many people compliment my daughter on her cuteness and beauty, and rightly so; she is very pretty. I often tell her, "Of course, you're a pretty girl. Your mother is gorgeous so you must be gorgeous as well." In other words, she is gorgeous because I am. Gorgeous is not something my daughter needs to live up to or attain; gorgeous is what she is already because it's what I am.

This is a rather flippant example, but it means the same as "Be perfect, just as your heavenly Father is perfect". Jesus may be saying you are already perfect for God, our Father, is perfect. If so, this is a statement of present fact not the starting pistol in a race to the finish line. Perfection need not be, and cannot be, attained. Perfection is what you are; there's nothing more to do.

And what is perfection anyway? At what point is something perfect? We can only declare something to be "perfect" if we have set standards, criteria and boundaries. Then we can declare, "Yes, it's perfect!" Without boundaries and limits how would you know when perfection has been attained? You wouldn't know. You could not know. And why must you know? It's attempting to know that appears to separate us from Creation. It's eating from the Tree, attempting to be as God and wanting to believe in the concept of "more" that clouds our vision. There is no more, we do not know, we have not separated ourselves and the Present has not abandoned us. Seeing this does not cause us to lose anything.

Questioning your judgments and considering other possibilities will not cause you to lose anything. You cannot lose what you never had.

PART III

SO WHAT?
IMPLICATIONS FOR REAL LIFE

As I was released from the prison of my own thinking, including the belief that there was an "I" who could think, I increasingly noticed my individuality. No longer a laundry list of separate things, labels and concepts, I can fully express myself with no worry of "should haves" and "shouldn't haves".

Limiting my freedom through judgment, and believing in order to attain "more", caused much fear and suffering. Now, there's no agenda, no expectation, no guilt and no goal. This doesn't mean that I am now running roughshod over little old ladies, robbing banks and kicking puppies; it simply means I remain aware of the Present. I'm aware there is only this moment and everything I will ever need is here now. But how does that help me in this life?

When I first began to explore this, I wondered what this had to do with anything. It's nice and all but will it help me sleep at night? Will it help me keep calm during my divorce proceedings? Will it lessen my impulse to just sit around and feel sorry for myself as I contemplate all the things that are wrong in my life? Yes, to all of these. By solving the problem where it is, in my mind, nothing outside needed to change. Yes the divorce is still happening and I'm still in a tiny apartment but it's all right. It's all in alignment. There is no mental opposition to what is, whatever it is. I still have preferences, I still experience surprise, anger, frustration, laughter and sadness, but it can be what it is in that moment then it can leave.

I've ceased trying to bring order to what I once thought was chaos. I've ceased trying to use belief in concepts as a bridge to get something more out of Life. Life is the treasure! Madly rummaging through the treasure looking for treasure was and is insane. I've called off the search for something better. The implications of this in my life are considerable.

The limited roles that I play as mother, wife, Christian, sibling and daughter are in the background where they were previously in the foreground and prominent drivers of my thoughts and behaviors. The foreground is this unchanging Present. The Present needs no direction, no help, no decision-making. It happens all by itself and it is in no way separate from me.

My roles still happen—they just happen without interference and my need to control the outcome. The outcome is already here and there's nothing more for me to do.

As a Mother

I have four fabulous and amazing children. My babies mean everything to me. I love them dearly but I see that just like everything else, my image of them is not the absolute truth. This is important to see as a mother because now I do not try to control them with my thoughts of who they should be. My children are just as complete, whole and present as I am. There's nothing I can or need do to improve them or make them better than they already are.

I don't speak to them very much about this but opportunities do arise from time to time. For instance, one day my daughter and I were discussing a girl in her school. I asked her, "Has anyone ever judged you at school?" She said, "Yes. Someone called me weird." I asked her how she felt when that person called her "weird". She said she felt "annoyed". I went on to explain to her that the assertion that she is "weird" was not about her; it was about the person who labeled her as "weird". I told her to imagine she was made of 1 billion parts, and because I'm her mother and so close to her, I know 25 parts out of the 1 billion. So when I tell Naomi that she's "pretty" or "smart" that is simply a judgment that reflects the extent of my ignorance.

Those labels have nothing to do with what or who she really is, and everything to do with the extent of my ignorance of who she really is. I told my 14-year-old that she is not "pretty" or "smart". When she looked at me with a frown on her face, I went on to explain this did not mean she was "ugly" and "unintelligent", it just meant that my labels don't define her. My labels are too small and too limited to define her actual magnificence.

The same goes for the girl who called her "weird". That girl knew, at most, 3 parts of the 1 billion parts that my daughter is made of. Her declaration that she is "weird" is totally a reflection of that girl's ignorance and has nothing to do with what my daughter is. This doesn't make that girl a bad or evil person. She is simply making a judgment, which she is responsible for. Because this declaration has absolutely nothing to do with Naomi, she need not see this girl as her enemy.

I also told Naomi that her very own thoughts about herself are simply a reflection of her ignorance as to who she really is. She's closer to herself than I am but she still only knows about 150 parts of the 1 billion parts that she's made of, so her thoughts about herself (and anyone else) are simply not the truth; "good" thoughts and "bad" thoughts. Any and all thoughts about her are not right, wrong, nice, mean, evil or holy. They're just untrue.

While my role as mom involves giving advice and explaining various aspects of life, my role as mom also involves learning from my whole and complete children. For example, there was an incident with my two youngest boys.

My boys love playing with LEGOs. For those of you who aren't familiar with LEGOs, they are colorful, interlocking, plastic blocks. My oldest son, who's 18 now, no longer asks for LEGOs for Christmas, but I guarantee if I decided to buy him a 3000-piece LEGO Bionicle set, he'd be overjoyed!

Of course, my youngest children still play with them. It warms my heart when they come to me and show me the things they've made with their blocks. They're so proud of their creations; and I'm proud of them for being so creative. Everything my 4-year-old makes is a Mega-something or other; a Mega car, a Mega tron, a Mega zoid, a Mega boat, etc. My 3-year-old isn't as interested in building things as his brother, but he will make something every now and then.

I remember one day I was in the kitchen washing the dinner dishes while they were in the den building with their LEGO blocks. They were playing quite nicely when suddenly I heard a terrible scream. It was the scream of a soul being violently wrenched from its body as it desperately tried to hold on. It was a scream filled with anguish, hopelessness and the darkest despair. My youngest had knocked over his brother's Mega Zoid. When I ran into the room, I saw my four-year-old's tear-filled eyes looking at his brother with a look of complete disbelief and total accusation. "What happened?!" I said. "He knocked down my Mega Zoid!" my-four-year-old yelled. He then walked over to his little brother's blocks and kicked them over. The fight was on. Before I could get to them, my youngest grabbed his brother's leg and was going in for the bite. My four year old has been bitten by his brother before, so all his efforts were on deflecting the incoming assault. "Stop it!" I yelled, as I tried to break them apart. Of course, they both calmed down and I did the mommy thing with time-outs and talks about being respectful of others' creations.

One of the many things I noticed in that moment was the differences in reactions. While my boys were going for each other's throats (as much as a three and four-year-old can) I was laughing. (I'm laughing now as I'm remembering the incident). My babies were sincerely upset by the incident while the entire situation was funny to me. The amount of passion and emotion displayed over LEGO blocks was hysterical. It was funny because I could see the bigger picture. I knew the Mega Zoid wasn't *really* a Mega Zoid (whatever that is); it was only a bunch of colorful LEGO blocks stacked atop one another. Mega Zoid was an idea that my four-year-old had created in his little mind. I knew it wasn't real. I knew it was just blocks that could be built again, maybe into an even more magnificent Mega Zoid; or into something completely different and even more creative! But to my son, the maker of this awesomeness, it was more than a bunch of colorful blocks, it was his fabulous creation; his unique idea.

My babies reminded me of something that day. My building blocks are Reality. My building blocks are the same as everyone else's building blocks; my mother's building blocks, my sister's, my brother's, my friend's and my enemy's building blocks.

Whatever it is that is the essence of all of us is what we use to create ourselves. We all have the same building blocks. My Mega Zoid is my image, my family, my possessions, my status, my intelligence, my religion, my lack of religion, my successes, my beliefs, and everything that makes up my idea of "me". It's all made of the same thing. It's an idea of a self, a family, intelligence, choices, problems, thoughts.

They're all ideas and I should respect and honor others' ideas of themselves. I now keep this in mind when I (in the form of someone else) kick and destroy an idea of myself. Instead of immediately getting angry I widen my perspective. I recognize the judgment I've made in that moment. I see that the truth of who I am has not been threatened, affronted or destroyed, because the truth of who I am is not an idea that can be believed then unbelieved. When my son kicked over the Mega Zoid that did not destroy the truth of what the Mega Zoid actually was... LEGO blocks. That truth remained unchanged. Regardless of what seemed to occur, the truth remained the same.

Finally, I remember one day driving my oldest son to the airport. As we were riding, we began discussing school. He told me, "Mom, I don't believe smart people know more, I just think they have a better memory... they simply remember better." I have to admit, I was slightly taken aback that my 16-year-old son had said something so wise and profound. He was spot on.

There is nothing new here. Creation is already done, and this is not something that can be learned or believed. It can only be seen. Remembering better is the process that allows us to see what's actually here. It helps us to remove the chains we've placed on ourselves, to finally see through a wider lens instead of through the very limited lens of belief that we're so afraid to relinquish.

But we do not lose anything by widening our perspective. Remembering better does not require loss or sacrifice. As my boys and my daughter grow, there will be many other opportunities for them to experience, learn and grow and for me to do the same.

Motherhood has certainly been a powerful way for me to look at my judgments of myself and to question the reliability and validity of those judgments. As a mother, it's also been very difficult to relinquish control, especially when it appears as if my children are not going in the direction I want them to go. This, coupled with what seems to be others' judgments of the decisions I make as a mother, tempts me to call on my own knowledge and understanding to save me from the loss of my role as mother. But it's at these times when I'm tempted to believe my judgments, when I see no one is judging me. If there is judgment, I am the one and only judge in this situation so I am responsible for the effects of that judgment. Whether the effect is anger, sadness, fear, happiness, joy or love, I am the cause.

As a mother, I will continue to raise my children, provide for them and love them as only a mother can, while at the same time knowing that there is really nothing for me to do. While change seems to happen, my children don't need to change and they cannot be improved. They are already perfect—as am I.

Chapter 2

As a Wife

I'm in the midst of my second divorce. Apparently I just can't get it right. We're calling it quits. The divorce process can be horrible; especially the feelings of uncertainty, anger, frustration and anxiety. Some men are such a pain. I know they're not all bad, but some of them clearly weren't raised right; which, of course, means it's not my fault. This is what I wanted to believe and I can believe this if I choose to.

Ending a relationship (any relationship) is horrible. It feels like you're losing something. Whether it's a good relationship or a bad relationship; whether it's a good loss or a bad loss, ending it feels like a connection has been severed; most of the time it hurts. I feel the anxiety, I feel the fear, I feel the anger and I feel the consequences of this loss, but I know this is not the absolute truth. This is not what is really going on.

The bottom line is, I was in a relationship, and it didn't work out. I had a plan, but it didn't work out. I had hopes, and they were dashed. I had dreams, and they were crushed. The relationship is over. Not the relationship between me and my husband, but the relationship between me and my life.

Both are concepts that I've created and believed in. Life is always changing and it's painful when we try to control it or hold onto it. Despite the instability and ever-changing-ness of "my life" sometimes it seems as if I'm able to hold onto something, like another person... a husband, a child or a friend, for instance. Finally, some stability! Then, they leave, they die or they reject me. Of course, I'm angry, depressed, anxious and fearful when this happens. It hurts when part of my life is taken away from me. The loss and pain I feel when a relationship is severed is my life, once again, slipping through my fingers. It's, once again, my inability to "keep it together".

So what can I do about it? How can I stop all these losses? How can I hold onto happiness in the relationship between me and my life? I cannot. I can only see that my belief is not the truth. I never *had* a husband. He never belonged to me. He was never mine to control, change and mold into what I wanted. I cannot lose something that I never had in the first place.

While going through this divorce, I've seen that at any given time my husband is doing the exact same thing that I'm doing. If I am seeking for truth then so is he, so we are each other's enemy. If I have seen through the illusion then so has he; and we're both simply looking at life unfold. It's like looking in a mirror. We're the same. There is no relationship because there are not two things. I do not have a relationship with my mirror image because we're the same thing, we arise together. I cannot be separate from my image and my image cannot be separate from me. The judgments and beliefs that create the concept called a "husband" are my mirror image. I am not separate from those judgment and beliefs; they are me.

The feelings that arise when I see or think of my "husband creation" are welcome and embraced. They are feelings based on judgments that I've made. The hurt is me, the pain is me, the anger is me and the frustration is me! I had to see that if hurt and pain is what I want, then my judgment will manufacture that for me. Simply seeing that process and allowing those feelings to be whatever they are is quite freeing. Seeing that I am the cause, and not something or someone outside of me, helps release me from a prison of beliefs that I'd created. At some point belief in judgments is unnecessary and is seen as quite useless. Whatever is present is present without a label or judgment.

My role as a wife has delved into the deepest and darkest recesses of myself and revealed many beliefs and judgments that I have tried to hide. But healing cannot occur unless these things are brought to the surface, and I am grateful to this creation called "husband" for doing that. At some point I had to stop denying and start admitting. It was a painful process and I'm not done yet. It has gotten easier since I am no longer pulling the wool over my own eyes.

I'm still following through with the divorce since that seems to be the way things are moving, but I trust life. Life knows what it's doing. As a wife, there's nothing for me to do in this situation, except look. Doing happens. Everything is taking care of itself; without my interference.

Chapter 3

As a Sibling

I have the best, most loving siblings in the world. I am grateful every day for my brother and sisters. I mentioned that I grew up as a Christian, well so did the rest of my siblings. Many of my family have very strong beliefs in God and His role in their lives. While my brother is not what I would call a devout Christian, in varying degrees my three sisters are.

I adore all my siblings and I respect their beliefs and their freedom to believe any and everything they wish to believe. I don't try to change them in any way. They are exactly what they are and what they are is perfection. They don't need to change their thinking or their beliefs.

Seeing this allows me to listen and simply be available to them without judgment and expectation. It is tough at times to hear talk of the Devil and hope for a better future and punishment of sinners, but this is my problem, not theirs. Everything they are is wholly in alignment with Life. I am the one who judges what I hear as problematic, so this is something that I must notice. In those situations, I see that I can't fix what isn't broken; in fact, the effort to fix it creates brokenness.

Because what I've written in this book is contrary to what they believe, I must admit that I was a little worried that they would see and treat me differently, but I have not experienced that. While there have been challenges and painful moments, my role as sibling seems to be a little more "cushy" than my role as a mother and wife. My "sibling space" seems to be more of a space of rest and reprieve. My brother and sisters are my go-to people when I need a good cry, a hug, an understanding ear and a laugh. They are totally awesome and words will never express just how much I love them or how much they love me.

My siblings help me to trust the process that is Life. They are very close to me and I can share things with them that I will not share with others. My conversations and interactions with them reveal childhood beliefs that my role as wife and mother may not reveal. The process of bringing these things to my awareness has been tremendously valuable.

Chapter 4

As a Daughter

Parents are very important to children: they're needed so we can blame someone for our problems. My father, Horace, died when I was six-years-old, but my mom, Patricia, is still with me. I don't remember much about my father except that he made me laugh and he let me do things that a six year old probably shouldn't do; like sitting on his lap and steering the car while he was driving or holding and attempting to shoot a loaded gun. After he died and when I was much older, I found out that my dad was an alcoholic and was most likely under the influence most of the time.

My mother is still here with me and I'm very happy about that. My mom is amazing and she is the most resilient and courageous woman I know. She's been through so much in her life but she always has a kind word and a thoughtful prayer when I need her.

Every conversation with my mom involves either

a talk of how this world will end soon and the return of Jesus Christ, or how we need to just hold on and everything will be alright in the next life.

My mom is a very devout Christian but she wasn't always this way. I remember her having several boyfriends after my father. I also remember moving a lot from one house to another. Stability was not something I was used to. My relationships with my father and mother would be a therapist's dream when compared to my own pattern of living. I can blame my parents six ways from Sunday as the primary cause of my poor decision-making and relationship choices. They could also blame their parents. My children could certainly blame me. Their children could, then, blame them, and on and on.

There's certainly plenty of blame to go around but to what end? What will blaming accomplish? Nothing. As a daughter, I see that I need to place the cause where cause belongs... solely with me. Knowing that I am the cause, releases my mom and dad while it also releases me. Now my mom is free to be who she is right now without being colored and tainted and limited by my judgments of her. Seeing me as the cause of my life choices empowers me and gives me courage to choose again. I can either believe my judgments of my parents or not. It's solely up to me, but I will experience the fruit that is borne of those judgments.

As a daughter, I no longer blame my parents' past for my present. I am grateful for my mom and dad

and gratitude allows me to simply live in the present
with confidence and ease

Chapter 5

As a Christian

In the conversations I've had with people about this message, everyone has asked what I currently believe. I understand that to feel safe we need to categorize and put labels on things. So for those of us that require a label, I'd have to say that I'm more of a Christian now than I've ever been.

I'm speaking of the Christianity that says God has only one Son. The Christianity that says "I and my Father are One". The Christianity that is wholly forgiving. There is no ambiguity in this Christianity; there are no questions and no confusion. What's confusing about One? As a Christian, I have to say that *the* most awesome and beautiful thing about this perception is that I can't get into Heaven alone. In other words, I can't be "saved" alone. Salvation is for all. For one to be delivered, all must be delivered because we're all God's one Son.

Relinquishing judgment breaks down mental walls that separate one thing from another, one person from another, and one experience from another. Without that mental boundary, there are no separate things. No separation *is* heaven. When I first discovered I had to take everyone with me to Heaven, I was furious. What do you mean, all must go with me? Do you know what he did to me? Do you know how he's treated me? Don't you know what she's put me through? What about the way they hurt my family? They don't get punished for that?! How can they go to Heaven too when they're guilty of all these things?! Don't you know that I'm so much better, I've done so much more, given so much more, helped so many more, prayed so much more, been through so much more than *they* have?! I get no reward?! No special treatment?! No mansion in Heaven?! What about all my sacrifice? Don't I get something for that!? What was the reason for my suffering and pain?! I could have been just as mean and nasty as my enemy and I could have still made it into Heaven?!

It's unfair! It's not right! It isn't just! What kind of God are you?! That's not what you said in the Bible! That's not what you've promised me! You're supposed to kill them! Punish them! Make them pay for all the wrong they've done! Throw them into Hell for not serving a loving God as perfectly as I did! I want to see their blood flow! Kill them! Punish them for not accepting your love into their black and evil hearts! Where's your army, your sword, your fire, your anger?!

Yes, I was livid. I truly believed that unconditional love had at least one condition, at least one limit. It couldn't really mean "without *any* conditions". But there are no limits in Love. Love is not made of separate aspects that can be taken away or lost. Love is whole and it accepts all. This means my neighbor is not limited and neither am I. We're both whole. I can love my neighbor as myself because my neighbor *is* myself; we are not separate.

As a Christian who was previously trying to live for—and please—a God that I had created with my own knowledge, I had to see that the only problem is in believing that love does have limits and can be separate. The solution to the one problem is seeing that separation isn't true. I was mistaken, I am not separate.

I don't have to punish myself for attempting to separate myself. All is forgiven because it never happened; I never succeeded in separating myself. The thing I hated, despised and wanted to punish was not my enemy; it was my judgment of myself as separate. As a Christian I forgive others and know that I am simultaneously forgiving myself because there are no "others". Ultimately it's seen that there is nothing to forgive, and this is true forgiveness.

As a human being

It appears as if this world is going to hell on roller skates. It appears as if human beings are destroying everything they touch or think about. Being a human being is all about every man for himself. It's all about what I can get with no regard for the feelings, safety or needs of other humans, other sentient beings or for the environment. We're like a virus infesting the planet voraciously consuming, and destroying any and everything it can until there is nothing left. That's what happened when I believed I was something called a "human being".

Before I questioned who I was, I needed more. I never could have enough. There was always more to get. I had to protect myself and provide for what was mine. There was never a moment or experience that did not revolve around me. I would listen to others' stories but unless it had something to do with me, I wasn't interested. If I did feign interest then the story was now about how interested, concerned, caring and present *I* was. It was still about me. I was the center of the universe.

Well, it's still about me, but the "me" is not the "me" that I thought it was. It's not a little limited human being that was born and will die. I am not that. As a human being, I can see that I am connected to everything around me. I am a whole part of the tapestry of this world. We are all here for and as each other. I am just as much a part of nature as the tree outside my window or the caterpillars that I detest so much. It's all "me" so I'm not superior to anything. I do not rule or have dominion over plants and animals. There is no hierarchy; we're all the same. As a human being, I no longer need to stand out in the crowd to find my place in this world or trample over everything in my path to leave a legacy for others to remember.

All I need do is be exactly who I am in this moment because this moment is the only moment there is. Recognizing this takes the pressure off me to make my "human being" story true. Making it true required a lot of suffering and pain. My "human being" story will never be true, and I've accepted and embraced that.

Now I can relate to others in a way that's honest because I've told the truth about myself. Behaviors will be whatever behaviors are and they are only seen and not judged. "Human being" is not the absolute truth and yet, here I am. What I am is a mystery but the fact that I am, is not. This is true for all. You cannot judge, "I am". You cannot believe "I am". And you cannot escape "I am".

Attempts to leave the present moment will always fail. When this is seen, the level of gratitude will surpass the highest level on the Richter scale. As a human being I have the perspective, educated language, humor and mental capacity to say, "Thank God for that!"

Chapter 8

Final Thoughts

Firing God was something that happened in the story of my life. What I fired was the story of Life that I'd created and believed in. That story is no longer working for me; in fact, it never worked for me!

Now that I see beliefs and judgments for what they are, non-threatening imitations of life, I'm no longer afraid, anxious or expectant. The voice in my head no longer has my full attention or participation. In fact, I barely notice it anymore because it's not about me and I'm perfectly okay with that.

As a relatively young African American female, I found myself in the company of many older white males (many with English accents) as I began this journey into finding who I really was. While listening to and appreciating every one of them, I wondered why that was. Where were the black people? First it was segregated bathrooms, schools, water fountains and buses. Now we have to stay at the bottom of the Consciousness level too?! We just can't get a break!

Of course color, race, gender, height, weight, geographic location, ethnicity, education level or spiritual background has absolutely nothing to do with what I'm communicating here. Nevertheless, our collective story makes distinctions in these and other ways. Well, I've just added a little sexy, brown-sugary southern Louisiana sweetness to the enlightenment pool. I hope that's okay. In any event, I'm meeting fabulous new people from all over the world of every race and ethnicity; every one of which has contributed to this book in some way.

As I said in the beginning, I have no story to tell that will give someone techniques to help them solve their problems, make more money, have higher self-esteem or get the man they really want. Much of what you've read here may seem to be nonsensical and irrelevant to "real life" and it is.

Real life is prior to what you've read here. Real life is prior to you and me. Real life does not need to be done. It requires no effort in any form.

You already know exactly what I'm communicating. It's seeing what I'm communicating for yourself that will make the difference; a difference that will leave you exactly where you are right now: whole, innocent and eternal.

ABOUT THE AUTHOR

Cheryl A. Abram is a mother of four and lives in Northern Virginia.

Visit Cheryl's website: www.cherylabram.com

Books *from* Non-Duality Press

If you enjoyed this book you might be interested in other titles published by Non-Duality Press.

Walking Awake, Steve Ford
The Best Thing That Never Happened, Joey Lott
Falling in Love With Where You Are, Jeff Foster
Dismantling the Fantasy, Darryl Bailey
Nothing to Grasp, Joan Tollifson
An Extraordinary Absence, Jeff Foster
The Wonder of Being, Jeff Foster
Only That: the Life and Teaching of Sailor Bob Adamson
Emptiness and Joyful Freedom, Greg Goode & Tomas Sander
Presence Volumes I & II, Rupert Spira
Oneness, John Greven
Awakening to the Dream, Leo Hartong
From Self to Self, Leo Hartong
Already Awake, Nathan Gill
Being: the bottom line, Nathan Gill
Perfect Brilliant Stillness, David Carse
I Hope You Die Soon, Richard Sylvester
The Book of No One, Richard Sylvester
Be Who You Are, Jean Klein
Who Am I?, Jean Klein
I Am, Jean Klein

CONSCIOUS.TV is a TV channel which broadcasts on the internet at www.conscious.tv. It also has programmes shown on several satellite and cable channels around the world including the Sky system in the UK where you can watch programmes at 8.30 pm every evening on channel No. 192. The channel aims to stimulate debate, question, enquire, inform, enlighten, encourage and inspire people in the areas of Consciousness, Non-Duality and Science. It also has a section called 'Life Stories' with many fascinating interviews.

There are over 200 interviews to watch including several with communicators on Non-Duality including Richard Bates, Burgs, Billy Doyle, Bob Fergeson, Jeff Foster, Steve Ford, Suzanne Foxton, Gangaji, Greg Goode, Scott Kiloby, Richard Lang, Francis Lucille, Roger Linden, Wayne Liquorman, Jac O'Keefe, Mooji, Catherine Noyce, Tony Parsons, Halina Pytlasinska, Genpo Roshi, Satyananda, Richard Sylvester, Rupert Spira, Florian Schlosser, Mandi Solk, James Swartz, Art Ticknor, Joan Tollifson, and Pamela Wilson. There is also an interview with UG Krishnamurti. Some of these interviewees also have books available from Non-Duality Press.

Do check out the channel as we are interested in your feedback and any ideas you may have for future programmes. Email us at info@conscious.tv with your ideas or if you would like to be on our email newsletter list.

WWW.CONSCIOUS.TV

Made in the USA
Lexington, KY
15 October 2015